"Relationships ge
other. Dana's mac
dive together and
           ROS

"The first thing I noticed (and loved) about Dana Nygaard's new book, *365 Dates to Renew Your Christian Marriage: Catholic Edition*, is that it's simple and amazingly easy to implement! It's just a quick and fun way to bring up interesting and important daily conversation starters that is sure to increase the love, intimacy and friendship between husbands and wives. I don't have time these days to read many books, but I certainly have 10 minutes each day to spend time with my wife discussing a few quick questions. Get the book, start the conversations and see your relationship improve!"

DAVE PALMER, Program Director for Guadalupe Radio Network and Author, *St. Thomas Aquinas for Everyone*

"In a world where couples have a hard time deciding where to go out to eat and struggle to stop looking at their phone, Dana has given a blueprint to bring communication and meaning back to date night. The questions in this book are thought-provoking and help couples use the limited time they have to open up to each other and share their inmost thoughts. Also, this book doesn't just have to be for date night. Couples could use these questions to talk at home in the evenings to connect every evening. I highly recommend this book."

CHRIS VAUGHAN, MA, Director of Marriage and Family Life, Diocese of Fort Worth, Texas

"Sue and I have read the book which reminded us of a Marriage Encounter that we made in 1972. As with your book, the theme is listening to one another with an open heart. This book reminded us that we need to keep an open heart and an open mind to one another's concerns through ongoing communication that leads to a deeper Union with each other and with Our Lord. This book deserves a rating of 5 stars out of 5."

DEACON PAUL AND SUSAN HUSTING, Diocese of Dallas, Texas

"The format of this workbook is so user-friendly and practical! It unwinds the journey of each couple with courage enough to take it up. It is filled with great guidance for each unique marriage, on how to use it or adapt it for their personal needs. Do not be afraid! Read, engage and renew your intimacy as a married couple."

SISTER MARY PAUL HAASE, religious sister,
Sisters of the Holy Family of Nazareth, Grand Prairie, Texas

"The title, *365 Dates to Renew Your Christian Marriage: Catholic Edition*, helps a couple to remember that every night could be considered a date night. Whether you're out on a date or at home or spending time together, making it special rather than 'ordinary'. This book initiates the creativeness for reflective conversation for couples who are struggling, and for those who feel that their marriage is strong. It allows a couple to move at their own pace, and is, and should be, a challenging way to reflect on the consent that you made at the time of your wedding day."

DEACON JIM AND SUSAN BINDEL, Diocese of Fort Worth, Texas

"Life was already full of busyness and then came 2020. As the world continues to spin out of control, now more than ever, married couples must set aside time for one another to strengthen their marriages. *365 Dates to Renew Your Christian Marriage: Catholic Edition* is a fabulous tool that will help husbands and wives gain the greatest benefit in that purposely scheduled time. Coming from years of expertise in counseling couples, Dana offers a practical guide to aid couples in the growth of their marriage, practically as well as spiritually. Schedule a date and enjoy the questions that will draw you closer to each other and closer to Our Lord."

ROBERT & DIANE SCHWIND, Three Hearts Institute

"Like anything else in life, our marriage requires constant renewal if it is to survive and thrive. Dana has come up with a simple, but effective way to do just that. By fostering a spirit of deep and personal sharing, she helps us to look into the mirror to discover God's work in us, in our spouse and in our relationship with one another. How so? By using the process that Jesus himself used all the time – the power of the question. I can't wait to start this with my wife. I hope you will make use of this fantastic resource as well!"

BRUCE R. BAUMANN, Director of Faith Formation,
Diocese of Dallas and Author, *Catholic to the Core*

"It is one thing to marry your beloved and vow before God to love and cherish each other till death do you part. But add on Dana's God-given ideas found in this book, and your marriage will go to a whole new level where it flourishes and the love between each other will grow stronger and sweeter each day. Thanks to Dana for her 'secret sauce' that's found in this creative and thoughtful book. If couples will embrace the concept of having real authentic conversations with each other, they will come to know and love their spouse even more than they thought imaginable."

DONNA WUERCH

"My wife and I will celebrate 25 years of marriage next year! We plan on using the *365 Dates to Renew Your Christian Marriage: Catholic Edition* by Dana Nygaard in the upcoming year. Dana Nygaard has written an easy-to-use date night resource that will change how married couples communicate with one another. After almost 25 years of marriage, I learn something new about my spouse when I engage her in fun, interesting and challenging questions. *365 Dates* takes all the work out of coming up with those questions. All we have to do is talk! Our world today is super distracted with media and technology. Put down your smartphone and pick up *365 Dates* to energize your conversation and renew your marriage. Marriage takes work, but *365 Dates* makes that work so much easier."

JAY WONACOTT, Director of the Office of Marriage and Family Life, Diocese of Boise

"I read this little gem from Dana Nygaard with such delight. As a marriage counselor and keen observer, marriage conversations for many do tend to become rather mundane. Busyness, financial and family concerns can lead couples to lose sight of the foundational relationship that makes any of it really matter. It's so easy to fall into complacency and practicality and lose sight of the treasure that is your spouse. Dana's format and questions are so refreshing and provide a simple, fun and effective way to give intimacy the little boost it may need. Grounded in her Catholic faith, Dana leads couples to a deeper intimacy and spiritual union so important for a lifelong happy marriage. I highly recommend picking up this gem and putting it into practice. You'll be happy you did!"

ALLISON RICCIARDI, LMHC, Founder and Director of The Raphael Remedy

"Dana Nygaard has provided a valuable tool to assist married couples who wish to grow closer to God together and to strengthen their Christian marriage. After the courting and honeymoon are over, life for married couples often revolves around hectic schedules, children, and the mundane activities of life. Time is a precious commodity and to make a marriage successful and spiritually fruitful, couples need to go the extra mile and intentionally break through to deeper, thought provoking questions which are the fertile ground for emotional growth. In her book, *365 Dates to Renew Your Christian Marriage: Catholic Edition*, she provides insightful, ready to go, questions that will spur on conversation, thought and a deeper love and appreciation for one another. Each date has three questions which she categorizes as, *Ready, Set and Go!* These questions are ready made for the beginning, middle and end of the date. The *Ready* question is an easy warm up question, the *Set* question is designed for some quality time together over a meal, and the *Go!* question is ideal for an after-dinner stroll or glass of wine. I highly recommend *365 Dates to Renew Your Christian Marriage* for it does the hard work of setting up the progression of questions and allowing the couple to respond with their head and their heart."

ALLAN F. WRIGHT, Author, *Daily Companion for Married Couples*

"Dana Nygaard is an experienced counselor and devout Catholic Christian. She works diligently to provide couples with the support they need to build and strengthen their relationships. Her new book, which is styled as a thought-provoking workbook, is called *365 Dates to Renew Your Christian Marriage: Catholic Edition*. This easy to use workbook will assist couples in sharing their personal ideas, feelings and hopes, and therefore build a stronger relationship."

FATHER BRUCE BRADLEY, Diocese of Dallas, Texas

CATHOLIC EDITION

365 Dates

TO RENEW YOUR
Christian Marriage

Increasing Your Emotional Intimacy
One Question at a Time

DANA NYGAARD, MA, LPC

Christian Comfort Counseling Publishing

Scriptures texts in this work are taken from the New American Bible, revised edition ©2010, 1991, 1986, 1970 Confraternity of Christian Doctrine, Washington, D.C., and are used by permission of the copyright owner. All Rights Reserved. No part of the New American Bible may be reproduced in any form without permission in writing from the copyright owner.

—

Imprimatur, given in Dallas, November 1, 2020,
by the Most Reverend Edward J. Burns, Bishop of Dallas

—

Photo Credit by Kenneth Munyer

365 Dates to Renew Your Christian Marriage:
Increasing Your Emotional Intimacy One Question at a Time
Catholic Edition
Published by Christian Comfort Counseling, PLLC
2201 Winterstone Drive
Plano, TX 75203
www.christiancomfortcounseling.com

This book or parts thereof may not be reproduced in any form, stored in a retrieval system, or transmitted in any form by any means – electronic, mechanical, photocopy, recording, or otherwise – without prior written permission of the publisher, except as provided by the United States of America copyright law.

Copyright ©2021 by Dana Nygaard, MA, LPC
All Rights Reserved

Acknowledgements

I WANT TO START by thanking my saintly husband, David Nygaard who inspired and encouraged me to write this book. He handled everything from household and business tasks to even the most minute details of our daily life so I could bring this project to fruition. He was as dedicated to completing this endeavor as I was. *My David*, I am blessed and highly favored to be your wife.

This book would not have been possible without the Holy Spirit that guided me through the entire process from inception to final editing.

I am grateful to Father James Yamauchi for his thoughtful and insightful foreword. Thanks go to Candace Bermender as my Marketing Director, who designed the beautiful cover and for her expertise at communication strategies. This project would not be what it is without the editing abilities of Leslie Cruzado who poured over each word of this book for countless hours. I am grateful to Tracy DuBois for the many phone conversations about the book structure. Much appreciation to Rachel Bower for graciously agreeing to test the questions with her sweetheart. I thank God for bringing each of you into my life as my brother and sisters in Christ.

To you, the reader. If you are reading this, it is because you desire to build the Kingdom beginning in your own marriage and for that I sincerely thank you.

"There are those who seek knowledge for the sake of knowledge - that is Curiosity.

There are those who seek knowledge to be known by others - that is Vanity.

There are those who seek knowledge in order to serve - that is Love."

St. Bernard of Clairvaux

Foreword

THE FIRST WORDS RECORDED OF JESUS in the Gospel according to St. John is a question He asks two men: "What do you seek?" (John 1:37). St. John the Baptist has proclaimed that Jesus is the Lamb of God and two disciples of the Baptist now begin to follow after our Lord. The public ministry of the Incarnate Son of God, who came to save His people from their sins, begins with a simple question to His first disciples.

In *365 Dates to Renew Your Christian Marriage*, Dana Nygaard provides Christian couples living in the modern world a simple and yet profound way to build upon their marital relationship through a series of questions. Some of these questions are easy to answer and may bring an instant smile to one's face, others are deep and offer the opportunity for reflection and, perhaps, a moment for some tears: all are designed for the couple, in the context of a secure and holy conversation, to come to a fuller knowledge, love, and service of each other through the sacrament of marriage they have received and now live amidst the crosses and blessings in each stage of married life. The fruit of these discussions will not only benefit the individuals, but it will strengthen the couple's relationship with God in their sacramental witness of the love between Christ and His Church, a love through which God continues to reveal Himself through the life and timeless teachings of the Church.

At the end of the Gospel according to John, after our Lord's Resurrection, the same two men to whom Jesus posed the question at the beginning of His public ministry were on a boat with some other disciples – they had fished all night and had caught nothing. As day was breaking, Jesus stood on the shore, though they did not recognize Him; listening to His instructions, they caught 153 large fish. The disciple who was present for the first words recorded in John's Gospel is now, through this miracle, able to tell Peter, "It is the Lord!" (John 21:7).

My prayer is that the Christian couples who have the discipline and the fortitude to regularly renew their Christian marriage with the help of these questions may, in the good times and the difficult times, always have the eyes to see and the ears to hear the Crucified and Risen Lord who is in their midst.

Father James Yamauchi, J.C.L.

Introduction

JANE FELT MORE ALONE THAN EVER. The silence in the car ride home was deafening. Her thoughts drifted back to just a few days ago when their marriage counselor gave them their first homework assignment - to go on a weekly date night. Jane's initial excitement was quickly tempered when the therapist instructed them to reconnect emotionally, *without* discussing their children.

As they drove to the restaurant for their first date night in years, they nervously laughed each time they inadvertently brought up the topic of their children. Their brittle laughter was replaced by a 'dry as dust' discussion on the pros and cons of replacing their ancient water heater. Jane was dismayed by how awkward it felt to be alone with her own husband. She was remembering their courtship when they could not seem to get enough of each other and would talk for hours on end. Jane was startled out of her reverie by her husband turning on the radio to fill the void in conversation.

The restaurant where they had a dinner reservation was known for its romantic ambiance, which gave Jane a flicker of hope that the evening could be salvaged. Upon being seated she scanned the room and felt a twinge of jealousy while watching enamored couples smiling and easily laughing at nearby tables. Jane refocused her attention on her husband and sighed deeply when she realized he was going on about which dental insurance plan to choose for their family.

The couple today who sits in front of the therapist is filled with renewed affection and tenderness towards each other. According to the therapist's notes in their file, Jane and her husband, had dramatically improved their emotional connection by intentionally seeking a deeper understanding and acceptance of their beloved.

This book will help your marriage by 'kick-starting' conversations that will make you laugh, reminisce and maybe even shed a tear or two as you uncover new insights into your spouse. By asking engaging questions and listening with an intent to love, you can invigorate your marital bond.

Years before I began working with couples as a Catholic Psychotherapist and leading marriage retreats, I became interested in keeping the proverbial flame alive in my own marriage. Our tradition on road trips was to bring two couples question books that we would take turns asking one another. This led to amazing conversations with new insight and humor into our relationship. There was one caveat though, time and time again we would come across questions that ranged from distasteful to inappropriate, and many were offensive to our Catholic sensibilities. On some trips we would reject question after question before finding one that we believed was appropriate for our sacred union.

This book was created to offer you the reader a safe and authentically Catholic experience as you endeavor to keep a fire burning in your relationship. The book is divided into 365 dates and each date includes a set of three unrelated questions. The sets of questions follow the format of *Ready, Set, Go!*

The *Ready* question is designed to start your date off on the right foot with a warm up question.

The *Set* question is meant to be discussed after you arrive at your date destination, while you enjoy a leisurely meal or perhaps in between games of bowling.

The *Go!* question is constructed for when you have some privacy after your date, while sharing a glass of wine on the patio of your home or taking a romantic stroll.

Each of the 365 dates revolve around the idea that they are a springboard to delve into each other's evolving interests, dreams, and life challenges. Allow these questions to take you down memory lane, into deep recesses and future ventures. Do not view this as a checklist but as a launching point to revive your emotional connection and renewed understanding of your beloved.

> *Hmmm...why are you still reading this introduction?*
> *Go ask your spouse for a date!*

A Little Guidance

I HAVE GATHERED some of the best questions together with you in mind. Each question has been thoughtfully, lovingly and prayerfully discerned. My hope is that you will answer each question with vulnerability and honesty. And that you receive your spouse's answers with enthusiasm, empathy, and tenderness. By doing so you will deepen your emotional intimacy and nourish your marriage. We suggest you do so by committing to one meaningful date a week with your spouse. Your weekly date can range from going out for a relaxing meal, organizing an exciting adventure, or creating a romantic stay-at-home date.

As with everything it is always wise to begin with prayer, so on page 19 you will find an individual prayer that you can say as you are preparing for your date. Followed by the Couple's Prayer which is meant to be prayed together prior to the date.

The process is to take turns asking and answering the three date questions, while allowing time to discuss each of your responses in greater depth. The questions are designed not as tasks to be completed, but as jumping off points.

Begin with the *Ready* question in order to start your date off on the right foot with an engaging yet easy discussion. This question could be talked about in the car as you drive to your date destination.

Follow up with the *Set* question once you have reached your destination and are able to focus on each other for a more personal conversation. This question is more substantial but one that can typically be discussed in a public setting.

Journey to a deeper conversation with the *Go!* question. By now, you should be primed for a more profound discussion that may require privacy. This conversation is structured to be shared in an intimate setting, where you feel free to be vulnerable.

Each *Ready, Set, Go!* question has a check box to mark off after you both have the opportunity to share your answer to the question. With all that in mind, adjust the book format to fit your unique personalities and lifestyle. You may choose to go through multiple dates on a road trip or set aside time daily to engage in conversation or we leave it to your own imagination.

*"And let them first pray together,
that so they may associate in peace."*
(St. Benedict)

Husband's Prayer (Based on Ephesians 5)
Dear Lord, help me to be a husband who loves my wife, just as Christ loves the Church. I ask for the grace to give my life for her each day. May I always enrich her life and bring her good. Amen.

Wife's Prayer (Based on Proverbs 31)
Dear Lord, help me to be a wife of noble character. I ask for the grace to be virtuous and capable. May I always enrich my husband's life and bring him good. Amen.

Couple's Prayer (Based on Ecclesiastes 4:12)
Dear Lord, we know that a cord of three strands is not quickly broken. We pray that in our marriage, as iron sharpens iron, we sharpen each other. Help us to submit to one another out of reverence for Christ. Give us the grace to love each other in an understanding way. Amen. Holy Family, pray for us!

This book is consecrated to the Holy Family

Date 1

☐ *Ready*   What one adjective best describes you?

☐ *Set*   If you could time travel to meet family members, would you rather go back in history or into the future?

☐ *Go!*   Would there be enough evidence to convict you if you were put on trial for your Catholic faith?

Date 2

☐ *Ready*   Which of us is more likely to laugh at an inappropriate time?

☐ *Set*   Is there something I could do daily to make your life easier or happier?

☐ *Go!*   What one thing would you change about our marriage?

Date 3

☐ *Ready*   Which of your childhood qualities have endured into adulthood?

☐ *Set*   What would you talk about in a 10-minute speech to the world?

☐ *Go!*   How do you live out the 'Golden Rule' in our marriage?

Date 4

☐ *Ready*   During elementary school, did you ever have to miss recess as a punishment?

☐ *Set*   What would you do if you knew you could not fail?

☐ *Go!*   Are you who you are today because of your parents or in spite of them?

Date 5

☐ *Ready*   What is your favorite guilty pleasure?

☐ *Set*   If you could have witnessed any biblical event, which one would you choose?

☐ *Go!*   What would you say in 3 words in a note to your younger self?

Date 6

☐ *Ready*   What would you like to be doing right now if money were not an issue?

☐ *Set*   Do you feel the need to be perfect?

☐ *Go!*   Are you overestimated or underestimated by others?

Date 7

- ☐ *Ready* — What makes you smile so hard that your cheeks hurt?

- ☐ *Set* — Who inspires you to be a better person?

- ☐ *Go!* — Is there a compliment you need to hear from me?

Date 8

☐ *Ready* — What world's largest collection would you like to own?

☐ *Set* — Is there something you have learned from a past relationship?

☐ *Go!* — How can I help make your life dreams come true?

Date 9

- [ ] *Ready* — What physical feature do you love most about me?

- [ ] *Set* — Is there something you wish you did better?

- [ ] *Go!* — When did you know you wanted to marry me?

Date 10

☐ *Ready* — How much would someone have to pay you to give up your favorite beverage?

☐ *Set* — During your childhood what activities or hobbies did you enjoy?

☐ *Go!* — What is your 30-second elevator speech about who you are as a Catholic?

Date 11

☐ *Ready* — What would you do with your time if you did not need to work for money?

☐ *Set* — How do you know that I am listening to you?

☐ *Go!* — Are there self-limiting beliefs that are holding you back from living your dream life?

Date 12

☐ *Ready* Is there a simple pleasure you are grateful for in life?

☐ *Set* What cause would your charitable foundation champion?

☐ *Go!* How do I make you a better person?

Date 13

☐ *Ready*   Who is the funniest person you know?

☐ *Set*   What 5 things (not people) are you most grateful for in your life?

☐ *Go!*   How do you want to be remembered?

Date 14

☐ *Ready* — Which one of your five senses would be the most difficult to live without?

☐ *Set* — Do you think it is important to discuss your feelings and not just your thoughts?

☐ *Go!* — What are some things that 'set the mood' for you?

Date 15

☐ *Ready*   If you could have any job in history, which would you choose?

☐ *Set*   What is the best compliment you have ever received?

☐ *Go!*   Which spiritual figures, living or deceased, have been the biggest influences in your faith?

Date 16

☐ *Ready* Who would you want to play you in a movie about your life?

☐ *Set* Which day would you choose to relive again and again?

☐ *Go!* What makes you feel appreciated by me?

Date 17

☐ *Ready* — If you could only use 2 beauty or toiletry products for the rest of your life, besides soap and shampoo, which ones would you choose?

☐ *Set* — What, if anything, do you miss about your childhood?

☐ *Go!* — Is there anything you wish you could unsee or unlearn?

Date 18

☐ *Ready* — Is there something that you are grateful for today that you did not have one year ago?

☐ *Set* — What are things you do not like but do anyway?

☐ *Go!* — Where do you see us in 5 years?

Date 19

☐ *Ready* — Who were the best and worst teachers you ever experienced?

☐ *Set* — What could I do to make you feel more understood?

☐ *Go!* — Has your life turned out as you expected?

Date 20

☐ *Ready* — When was the last time you laughed out loud?

☐ *Set* — What question would you most like God to answer?

☐ *Go!* — Is there something you would like to change about our marriage?

Date 21

☐ *Ready* — Are there any new family traditions you would like to start?

☐ *Set* — How can you improve your life by making one change?

☐ *Go!* — What do you most regret never telling someone?

Date 22

☐ *Ready*   Did you ever receive a detention or suspension from school?

☐ *Set*   What do you think is going right in our relationship?

☐ *Go!*   When do you feel respected by me?

Date 23

☐ *Ready* — When you were a teen what did you think about married life?

☐ *Set* — Am I good at supporting you when you are stressed?

☐ *Go!* — What life lesson did you learn the hard way?

Date 24

☐ *Ready* — If you could spend the night in a museum, which one would you choose?

☐ *Set* — How do you like me to express my love for you the most - words, gifts or touch?

☐ *Go!* — What is the biggest 'mistake' you have ever made in your life that turned out to be a blessing?

Date 25

☐ *Ready* — What language should we learn together?

☐ *Set* — Do you ever feel invisible with certain people or in certain situations?

☐ *Go!* — What role did God have in your childhood?

Date 26

☐ *Ready* — Have you ever disliked something and then changed your mind?

☐ *Set* — What brings you joy?

☐ *Go!* — Do I devote regular time to anything that you perceive as a possible threat to our marriage?

Date 27

☐ *Ready*   How did your parents meet?

☐ *Set*   What is your most proud moment from your childhood?

☐ *Go!*   Do you have any 'emotional baggage' you need to work through to be more at peace?

Date 28

☐ *Ready* — What was the biggest lie you ever told your parents?

☐ *Set* — Is there something in your life that is not working well?

☐ *Go!* — What about money scares you?

Date 29

☐ *Ready*   Have you ever called in sick when you needed a mental health day?

☐ *Set*   Whose respect have you earned?

☐ *Go!*   What helps you most when life gets hard?

Date 30

☐ *Ready* — Is there a trait you wish more Catholics would embrace?

☐ *Set* — What makes you feel valued?

☐ *Go!* — Is there something that never ceases to amaze you?

Date 31

☐ *Ready*   What restaurant would you choose to eat at the rest of your life?

☐ *Set*   Do you consider yourself to be a forgiving person?

☐ *Go!*   Is there a side of you that you do not often let others see?

Date 32

☐ *Ready* — Was there anything especially noteworthy about your birth story?

☐ *Set* — What travel location is at the top of your bucket list?

☐ *Go!* — When have you been judged unfairly?

Date 33

☐ *Ready* — Is there a movie or T.V. show you never tire of watching?

☐ *Set* — Did you experience peer pressure as a child or teen?

☐ *Go!* — What tests your patience to the limit?

Date 34

Ready — If you had to wear the wardrobe of a famous person, living or deceased, whose wardrobe would you choose?

Set — Is there something you want to do that I do not give you the opportunity to enjoy?

Go! — What has been the ultimate test of your physical or mental endurance?

Date 35

☐ *Ready*   What trivia game subject is your favorite to answer?

☐ *Set*   If a family member needed a kidney and you were the perfect match, would you donate your organ?

☐ *Go!*   Which 3 words come to mind when you think of God?

Date 36

☐ *Ready* — What is the dumbest way you have ever injured yourself?

☐ *Set* — Do you believe you are good at expressing gratitude?

☐ *Go!* — Were you ever bullied?

Date 37

☐ *Ready* — What job would you never do even for $1,000,000?

☐ *Set* — How did your parents embarrass you as a child?

☐ *Go!* — What is your fondest memory of our courtship?

Date 38

☐ *Ready* — Who in your family would you choose to start a business?

☐ *Set* — Do you find it difficult to say "no" to others?

☐ *Go!* — What are your best and worst habits?

Date 39

☐ *Ready* — What school course has been the most useful to you as an adult?

☐ *Set* — Is there something people would never know about you just by your appearance?

☐ *Go!* — How can I bring more romance to our marriage?

Date 40

☐ *Ready* — Would you rather eat without gaining weight or always get plenty of sleep?

☐ *Set* — Who in your life does not understand your Catholic faith?

☐ *Go!* — What life lessons do you wish you knew 10 years ago?

Date 41

☐ *Ready* — What modern technology, other than a cell phone, do you rely on now that you did not have as a child?

☐ *Set* — Who makes you feel appreciated, besides me?

☐ *Go!* — What was the hardest aspect of growing up for you?

Date 42

☐ **Ready** — During elementary school, what was the first thing you would do after arriving home?

☐ **Set** — If you were a talk show guest what would be the topic of conversation?

☐ **Go!** — What did your parents teach you about love and marriage?

Date 43

☐ *Ready* — What is the funniest thing you have recently seen?

☐ *Set* — Where would you go on vacation without money being a factor?

☐ *Go!* — Which parent did you go to as a child when you needed to talk?

Date 44

☐ *Ready* — What are the best and worst parts of traveling?

☐ *Set* — Is there something that gets better as you get older?

☐ *Go!* — Who is someone you have lost respect for that you once admired?

Date 45

☐ *Ready* — What was the most mischievous thing you did as a child?

☐ *Set* — Do you have a go-to scripture?

☐ *Go!* — As your spouse, do I fulfill your romantic longings?

Date 46

☐ *Ready* — What do you remember about our first road trip together?

☐ *Set* — If you could start your career over, what would you do differently?

☐ *Go!* — When is it difficult for you to be open with me?

Date 47

☐ *Ready* — What job do you think you would have if you had lived in the early 1900's?

☐ *Set* — Were you encouraged to be close to your family members?

☐ *Go!* — How are you different from most people?

Date 48

☐ *Ready* — Which famous artist, living or deceased, would you commission for a portrait?

☐ *Set* — Have you ever wanted to write a book?

☐ *Go!* — What have I done recently that made you feel proud in front of others?

Date 49

☐ *Ready* — If you had unlimited resources, what would you build or create?

☐ *Set* — What is the best compliment I have ever given you?

☐ *Go!* — How would you finish this sentence, "I love when you ___"?

Date 50

☐ *Ready* Did you have a favorite family tradition during your childhood?

☐ *Set* Who that you know, would you trade jobs for one day?

☐ *Go!* Have you ever felt like Job in the Bible?

Date 51

☐ **Ready** — Is there a household chore that you wish you never had to do again?

☐ **Set** — What is the most adventurous thing you have ever done?

☐ **Go!** — Are you holding any grudges against me?

Date 52

☐ *Ready* — Is there a word that best describes my parents?

☐ *Set* — What contrast between us do you love?

☐ *Go!* — Are there times when I overstep boundaries by criticizing versus expressing a reasonable complaint?

Date 53

☐ *Ready*   What do you like most about your appearance?

☐ *Set*   Which award would you nominate your mother or father for their legacy?

☐ *Go!*   As a child, what scared you?

Date 54

☐ *Ready* — Which one of our vacation spots would you choose to live?

☐ *Set* — What is the scariest place you have ever visited?

☐ *Go!* — Is there something you need more of in your life?

Date 55

☐ *Ready*   What qualities do you most admire in a priest?

☐ *Set*   Do you focus more on the past, present or future?

☐ *Go!*   Is there a memory of me that always makes you laugh?

Date 56

☐ *Ready* — At an event, would you rather be underdressed or overdressed?

☐ *Set* — Is there anything you would not want to share with your family of origin?

☐ *Go!* — Do you have a physical feature that makes you self-conscious?

Date 57

☐ *Ready* — Would you rather ask or answer questions?

☐ *Set* — What have been significant milestones in our marriage?

☐ *Go!* — Ten years from now what accomplishments would you like to have personally achieved?

Date 58

☐ *Ready*   What is the most boring job you can imagine?

☐ *Set*   How have service and charity played a role in your life?

☐ *Go!*   Do I do enough to encourage you?

Date 59

☐ *Ready* — If we won the lottery, how would our lives change?

☐ *Set* — Is there anything you disliked from your childhood, but can now appreciate?

☐ *Go!* — How do you show your love for me?

Date 60

☐ *Ready* What is a favorite memory of a pet or animal?

☐ *Set* How do you show strangers the love of Christ?

☐ *Go!* Does talking about our physical intimacy make you uncomfortable?

Date 61

☐ *Ready* — Have you ever been completely surprised at receiving something for free?

☐ *Set* — What is the bravest thing you have ever done?

☐ *Go!* — On a scale of 1-10, with 10 being high, how happy are you with our marriage during this season of our lives?

Date 62

☐ *Ready* What is the most outrageous behavior you have ever personally witnessed?

☐ *Set* Are there character traits that you inherited from your grandparents?

☐ *Go!* How do I respond when you are righteously upset with me?

Date 63

☐ *Ready* — What age do you feel?

☐ *Set* — Is there anything you wish you could do better?

☐ *Go!* — Do you think I focus more on your flaws or attributes?

Date 64

☐ *Ready* — What is something that brings an instant smile to your face?

☐ *Set* — Would you like to live past the age of 100?

☐ *Go!* — How have you blessed our marriage?

Date 65

☐ *Ready*   Where would you like to have a peek 'behind the scenes'?

☐ *Set*   Has your journey as a Catholic been a straight or winding path?

☐ *Go!*   What is your earliest childhood memory?

Date 66

☐ *Ready* — Is there anything you desire to be the best at in the world?

☐ *Set* — If you never made a penny from your efforts what would you do anyway?

☐ *Go!* — What energizes and encourages you the most?

Date 67

☐ *Ready*   Have you ever wanted to object at a wedding?

☐ *Set*   What is the most embarrassing moment of your life?

☐ *Go!*   Am I responsive to your bids for my attention?

Date 68

☐ *Ready* — What would you sell if you had an infomercial?

☐ *Set* — Is there a law you would like repealed?

☐ *Go!* — What is the worst emotional or mental anguish you have ever endured?

Date 69

☐ *Ready* — Would you rather be a lawyer or a judge?

☐ *Set* — Is there a favorite story about your life that you enjoy telling?

☐ *Go!* — What are your retirement dreams?

Date 70

☐ *Ready* — If you were forced to get a tattoo, what would you choose?

☐ *Set* — What do you do that always brings a smile to my face?

☐ *Go!* — Is there a time when you were hurt, and God brought you to forgiveness?

Date 71

☐ *Ready* — What makes you roll your eyes?

☐ *Set* — If the President needed you for a special project, what expertise could you offer?

☐ *Go!* — Would you ever want to move from where we currently live?

Date 72

- [ ] *Ready* — Was there a chore or activity in your childhood that you detested?

- [ ] *Set* — Is there something that people ask you often?

- [ ] *Go!* — What is the best part of being married?

Date 73

☐ *Ready*   What makes people look ridiculous that they think makes them look good?

☐ *Set*   How would you describe a perfect day?

☐ *Go!*   Are you ever disappointed when you seek me out for emotional support?

Date 74

☐ *Ready* — Which jobs would you not be good at performing?

☐ *Set* — Are you known for your generosity?

☐ *Go!* — How would you complete the following sentence, "Our marriage would be blessed if we ___?"

Date 75

☐ *Ready* — Do you sometimes dance even without music?

☐ *Set* — What are your thoughts on the Charismatic Renewal in the Catholic Church?

☐ *Go!* — How do you emotionally experience my love for you?

Date 76

☐ *Ready* — Does hearing the music from an ice cream truck make you smile?

☐ *Set* — What topic would you choose for a documentary?

☐ *Go!* — Is there an aspect of our marriage that makes you feel sad or disappointed?

Date 77

☐ *Ready* — Would you prefer a lake or beach house?

☐ *Set* — Can you tell me your life story in 2 minutes or less?

☐ *Go!* — What marital lesson took you the longest to learn?

Date 78

☐ *Ready* — What is your oldest personal possession?

☐ *Set* — If you were the President, what is the first executive order you would institute?

☐ *Go!* — Do you feel secure in our relationship?

Date 79

☐ *Ready* — Do you consider yourself to be low or high maintenance?

☐ *Set* — Would you rather fail or never try?

☐ *Go!* — What is an unpopular opinion you hold?

Date 80

☐ **Ready** — What is something you tell yourself you will do when you retire or have more time?

☐ **Set** — Which person has been the biggest influence in your life?

☐ **Go!** — Are you focused on your relationship with Jesus or are you distracted by worldly pursuits?

Date 81

☐ *Ready*   If we had to enter a witness protection program, what would you choose for a name and where would you like to live?

☐ *Set*   What were you born to do?

☐ *Go!*   Am I consistently treating you as the most important person in my life?

Date 82

☐ *Ready* — Who besides me, is your favorite person in the world?

☐ *Set* — What would you do if you did not care what others thought?

☐ *Go!* — Am I attentive to your sexual needs?

Date 83

☐ *Ready* — Which fashion trend would you like to see return and which would you like to disappear?

☐ *Set* — How can you tell if someone is lying to you?

☐ *Go!* — What are the 3 happiest moments of your life?

Date 84

☐ *Ready* — What world record would you like to break?

☐ *Set* — Which qualities do you admire in other people?

☐ *Go!* — Am I ever defensive towards you?

Date 85

☐ *Ready* — What made your best friend from childhood so special?

☐ *Set* — Where is your favorite place on earth?

☐ *Go!* — What prayer are you still hoping God will answer?

Date 86

- [ ] *Ready* — If you could instantly be great at an Olympic sport, which would you choose?

- [ ] *Set* — Where do you like to go when you need some alone time?

- [ ] *Go!* — Do we approach our marriage with a 'we' or 'me' outlook?

Date 87

☐ *Ready* — If you did not have access to your cell phone for a month, what would you miss most?

☐ *Set* — Do you think we spend enough time together as a couple?

☐ *Go!* — Is my love for you obvious to you and others?

Date 88

☐ *Ready* — Would you rather speak 7 languages fluently or be a genius with musical instruments?

☐ *Set* — How do you see your role in our relationship?

☐ *Go!* — With what would you want a second chance?

Date 89

☐ *Ready* — Have you ever laughed so hard that you wet your pants?

☐ *Set* — If you were going to bury a time capsule, what would you include?

☐ *Go!* — What could we do as a couple to better love the people around us?

Date 90

☐ *Ready*   What childhood candy or treat, did you enjoy the most?

☐ *Set*   Is there an area of our Catholic faith where you would like us to delve deeper?

☐ *Go!*   Do we demonstrate mutual respect?

Date 91

☐ *Ready*   If this stage of our life were a country song, what would be the title?

☐ *Set*   What gives you a sense of belonging to a group?

☐ *Go!*   In what circumstances do you feel closest to me?

Date 92

☐ *Ready* — If you had to teach a course, what would you teach?

☐ *Set* — Is there something on your bucket list that may surprise people?

☐ *Go!* — What is the area of my life where you have seen the greatest growth?

Date 93

☐ *Ready*   Do you have a celebrity doppelganger?

☐ *Set*   How would you dress me for a date night?

☐ *Go!*   What do you enjoy most about my company?

Date 94

☐ *Ready* — What event would you like to attend if you had V.I.P. access?

☐ *Set* — Are my hugs too short, too long, or exactly right for you?

☐ *Go!* — Do I respect your knowledge in decision making?

Date 95

☐ *Ready*   If you endorsed a current commercial brand, which one would you choose?

☐ *Set*   What strengthens your faith?

☐ *Go!*   Are you satisfied with the frequency and quality of our physical intimacy?

Date 96

Ready — When was the last time I made you laugh?

Set — Is there something that you have never done but would like to do?

Go! — What do I mean to you?

Date 97

☐ **Ready** — What is something that frightens other people but does not scare you?

☐ **Set** — On what topics do you see yourself as an expert?

☐ **Go!** — How do you protect and defend what is important to you?

Date 98

☐ *Ready* — What do you geek out about the most?

☐ *Set* — Is there something you would like to invent?

☐ *Go!* — How do people feel after spending time with you?

Date 99

☐ *Ready*   What have you become bored of recently?

☐ *Set*   How can I pamper you more?

☐ *Go!*   What difficult situations did you overcome as a child?

Date 100

- [ ] **Ready** — If you owned a retail store, what would you sell?

- [ ] **Set** — What is something you would like to do more often together?

- [ ] **Go!** — Do you think others view our marriage as sacred and holy?

Date 101

☐ *Ready* — Has anyone ever saved your life?

☐ *Set* — What is the most awkward social situation you have ever experienced?

☐ *Go!* — Is there a fear you would like to overcome?

Date 102

☐ *Ready* — Who would you like to shadow for a day?

☐ *Set* — Are you too quick or slow to trust people?

☐ *Go!* — Was there someone in need of assistance that you now regret not helping?

Date 103

☐ *Ready* — Would you rather hear good or bad news first?

☐ *Set* — What motivates you to do your best?

☐ *Go!* — Do you believe at times I stonewall you?

Date 104

☐ *Ready* — Which would be worse a noisy or nosy neighbor?

☐ *Set* — What is something you look forward to in our future?

☐ *Go!* — Is there something I do that drives you crazy?

Date 105

☐ *Ready*   Is there a personal item you often misplace?

☐ *Set*   What are 3 things you really appreciate that I do for you and our family?

☐ *Go!*   Do you feel there is a spiritual void in our life that God is calling us to fill?

Date 106

- [ ] **Ready** — Have you ever lost an item that is irreplaceable?

- [ ] **Set** — What unique thing about me do you find endearing?

- [ ] **Go!** — Do you feel that you are emotionally safe to be vulnerable with me?

Date 107

☐ *Ready* — Would you rather be alone on a deserted island or have someone with you who never stopped talking?

☐ *Set* — What was your first impression of me?

☐ *Go!* — Are we growing towards or away from each other?

Date 108

☐ *Ready* — What is the worst movie you have ever watched?

☐ *Set* — If you could spend 24 hours doing anything with me, what would you choose?

☐ *Go!* — In what area of our relationship do you need me to extend more patience and flexibility?

Date 109

☐ **Ready** — If you curated a museum, what famous items would you want to display?

☐ **Set** — What is something you never want me to change about myself?

☐ **Go!** — Do you perceive that there are any aspects of my life that are off limits to you?

Date 110

☐ *Ready* — What scents or smells bring you comfort?

☐ *Set* — Besides the Bible, what are your favorite Catholic books?

☐ *Go!* — Do you believe that you make a good effort to meet my needs?

Date 111

☐ *Ready* — What about me first attracted you?

☐ *Set* — Are you insecure about yourself in any way?

☐ *Go!* — What should I know about you that I have never thought to ask?

Date 112

☐ *Ready* — What Halloween costumes did you wear as a child?

☐ *Set* — Have you learned anything from observing other people's marriages?

☐ *Go!* — Would you say we love each other more or less than when we first married?

Date 113

☐ *Ready* — If we started a duo music group, what would we name our band?

☐ *Set* — What is the best part of spending time together?

☐ *Go!* — When do you truly feel alive?

Date 114

☐ *Ready*   What one word best describes our marriage?

☐ *Set*   In what ways do you think we love differently?

☐ *Go!*   Do you like the person you have become?

Date 115

☐ **Ready** — Which game show do you think you could win?

☐ **Set** — Who besides me has God put into your life for a specific reason?

☐ **Go!** — How can I add more value to our quality time together?

Date 116

☐ *Ready* — Have you ever been helped by a self-help book?

☐ *Set* — What are your top 2 pet peeves?

☐ *Go!* — Is there something specific I did recently that made you feel loved, honored and respected?

Date 117

☐ *Ready* — What is the best prank you have ever played on someone?

☐ *Set* — Have you ever marched for or against a cause?

☐ *Go!* — In what ways do we work well together?

Date 118

☐ **Ready** — If you bought a yacht, what would you name her?

☐ **Set** — Do we place a similar value on leisure time activities?

☐ **Go!** — What is something you wish I understood more about you?

Date 119

☐ *Ready* — Would you ever participate in a reality T.V. show?

☐ *Set* — What important lesson did you learn outside of a formal education?

☐ *Go!* — Am I putting less important things ahead of our marriage?

Date 120

☐ *Ready* — What would you choose as a superpower if you were a superhero for a day?

☐ *Set* — During your childhood, what happened at a typical mealtime?

☐ *Go!* — Was there ever a prayer you genuinely wanted but were later relieved that God did not answer?

Date 121

☐ *Ready* — Who, living or deceased, would you like to invite to a dinner party?

☐ *Set* — How do you get yourself out of a bad mood?

☐ *Go!* — Is there anything you have not shared with me that keeps you awake at night?

Date 122

☐ *Ready* — What magazine would you be chosen for the front cover?

☐ *Set* — Do you think about me during the day?

☐ *Go!* — What leads to you becoming overwhelmed?

Date 123

☐ *Ready* — What theme song should be played every time you enter a room?

☐ *Set* — Is there anything you feel shy about with me?

☐ *Go!* — What are your core values and are you being true to them?

Date 124

☐ *Ready* — Is there a word that sums up the internet?

☐ *Set* — What is the best thing I did for you on a special occasion?

☐ *Go!* — Are we growing together or apart regarding our values and morals?

Date 125

☐ *Ready* — Is there a sacred hymn or praise and worship song that brings you peace and joy?

☐ *Set* — What is something you procrastinate on regularly?

☐ *Go!* — How can you tell when I am happy?

Date 126

☐ *Ready* — How would you describe your entire life in a single sentence?

☐ *Set* — Is it difficult for you to disagree with others?

☐ *Go!* — What important change do you believe I need to make in my life that I am avoiding?

Date 127

☐ *Ready* — Would you accept an opportunity to travel in space?

☐ *Set* — What do you want to do but can never find the time?

☐ *Go!* — How can we improve our conflict resolution skills?

Date 128

☐ *Ready* — If stranded on a deserted island, what 3 material items would you want?

☐ *Set* — When you were growing up, who were you closest to in your family?

☐ *Go!* — How do you feel about taking breaks when our discussions get too emotionally overwhelming?

Date 129

☐ *Ready* — What famous movie would you choose to star in if it were made into a remake?

☐ *Set* — Would you be open to attending a yearly couple's retreat?

☐ *Go!* — How do you prefer I communicate a complaint about our relationship?

Date 130

☐ *Ready* — How would you spend a year of paid leave?

☐ *Set* — What do you miss now that we used to do together?

☐ *Go!* — Which of the 10 Commandments do you struggle with the most?

Date 131

☐ **Ready** — What could you do for hours on end and not consider a waste of time?

☐ **Set** — If you could rewrite history, what significant world event would you change?

☐ **Go!** — How would you rate our ability to compromise in our relationship?

Date 132

☐ *Ready* — How is our marriage like an adventure?

☐ *Set* — During your upbringing, did you have to follow any unusual or strange rules?

☐ *Go!* — Do I handle my daily stressors well or take them out on you?

Date 133

☐ *Ready* — What song reminds you of me?

☐ *Set* — How do you react under immense pressure?

☐ *Go!* — Do I overuse the words "always" and "never"?

Date 134

☐ *Ready* — Do you have a strange habit?

☐ *Set* — When are you at your happiest?

☐ *Go!* — What strong emotions do you feel on a regular basis that are not bearing good fruit?

Date 135

☐ *Ready* — Who would you like to sing a duet with if you could pick anyone in the world?

☐ *Set* — What is the kindest thing a family member has ever done for you?

☐ *Go!* — Have you ever struggled to entrust your life to God's plan?

Date 136

☐ *Ready* — Is there a belonging of mine that you wish would just disappear?

☐ *Set* — Do you wish you had put more effort into your education?

☐ *Go!* — What personality trait would you like to improve?

Date 137

☐ *Ready* — What hobby would you like to begin?

☐ *Set* — Is there a popular childhood story about you that your parents like to tell?

☐ *Go!* — What can lead you to feel sad?

Date 138

☐ **Ready** — What is your favorite physical feature of mine?

☐ **Set** — Do you equate 'being emotional' with 'being out of control'?

☐ **Go!** — Is there anything you have asked me to do that I have neglected?

Date 139

☐ *Ready* — What is the most daring thing you have done in your life?

☐ *Set* — Who would you like to get to know better?

☐ *Go!* — Do your thoughts ever lead you to experience attacks of shame?

Date 140

☐ *Ready*   In the next few weeks, what adventure would you like us to do together?

☐ *Set*   What is a waste of money according to you?

☐ *Go!*   How do you envision hell?

Date 141

☐ **Ready** — Where do you do your best thinking?

☐ **Set** — How do you feel the most connected to me intellectually?

☐ **Go!** — Do you believe I ever express contempt towards you?

Date 142

☐ *Ready* — Would you ever consider running for public office?

☐ *Set* — What expressions or phrases did your mother and father often say during your childhood?

☐ *Go!* — Do you express or repress your emotions?

Date 143

☐ *Ready* — What song always gets you out on the dance floor?

☐ *Set* — Were there any playground activities you especially liked as a child?

☐ *Go!* — Do you carry bitterness towards anyone, including yourself?

Date 144

☐ *Ready* — What are the best and worst parts of traveling?

☐ *Set* — Is there anything you learned from your first job?

☐ *Go!* — What is the most dangerous thing you have ever done?

Date 145

☐ *Ready*   Is there an activity that instantly calms you?

☐ *Set*   Have I impacted your walk with the Lord?

☐ *Go!*   What question have you always wanted to ask me but have not?

Date 146

☐ *Ready* — Who was your first crush and was the affection reciprocated?

☐ *Set* — Would you rather spend a day with your kindergarten self or your elderly self?

☐ *Go!* — What do you know about your parent's upbringing?

Date 147

☐ *Ready* — Do you wish we would travel more or less as a couple?

☐ *Set* — When you look at me do you see a spouse who deeply loves you?

☐ *Go!* — What has been your most vulnerable moment in our relationship?

Date 148

☐ *Ready* — What do you wish you could still do that is not socially acceptable as an adult?

☐ *Set* — When was the last time you cried?

☐ *Go!* — Is there a time when you wish you had been more careful with your words?

Date 149

☐ *Ready* — What flower makes you think of me?

☐ *Set* — Is there something you have thrown away and regretted?

☐ *Go!* — Are there any of your friendships that may be unhealthy for you?

Date 150

☐ **Ready** — If you were a teacher, what subject would you teach?

☐ **Set** — What advice would you give a person converting to Catholicism?

☐ **Go!** — Do the people you love most know how much you love them?

Date 151

☐ **Ready** — What are the best and worst things about being an adult?

☐ **Set** — In school, were you a leader or follower?

☐ **Go!** — What is unique about our relationship compared to others?

Date 152

☐ *Ready*   At a party, where can someone find you?

☐ *Set*   Were you an early or late bloomer regarding puberty?

☐ *Go!*   Are there any charitable organizations you would like us to bequeath to in our wills?

Date 153

☐ *Ready* — Did you have a special or secret place to play as a child?

☐ *Set* — How do you think others view you?

☐ *Go!* — Were you chosen first or last when picked for sports teams in P.E. class?

Date 154

☐ **Ready** — What is the worst name for a pet you have ever heard?

☐ **Set** — Do you usually think or speak first?

☐ **Go!** — What mistakes have you made that you still have not forgiven yourself?

Date 155

☐ *Ready*   What is an ideal weekend for you?

☐ *Set*   Has your family ever pressured you to behave in a certain way?

☐ *Go!*   What do Saint John Paul II's words from the Angelus, "We are an Easter People and Alleluia is our song!" mean to you?

Date 156

☐ *Ready* — If you had to spend $1,000,000 in one day, what would you buy?

☐ *Set* — What is something you wish I would ask you more often?

☐ *Go!* — Do you need to seek my forgiveness for anything?

Date 157

☐ **Ready** — Did you visit your parent's workplace during your childhood?

☐ **Set** — Do you unfairly compare yourself to others?

☐ **Go!** — Is there something in your life you need less of now?

Date 158

☐ *Ready* Of all the restaurants that we have been to together, which is your favorite?

☐ *Set* Do you have enough time to enjoy your hobbies?

☐ *Go!* How would your life change if you overcame any self-limiting fears?

Date 159

☐ *Ready* — Which animal would you like to ride on at least once in your lifetime?

☐ *Set* — Are there any steps you could take to simplify your life?

☐ *Go!* — Were you encouraged as a child to express your needs?

Date 160

☐ *Ready* — Did you ever make up a secret handshake or language with a friend, and do you still remember it?

☐ *Set* — What would your autobiography be titled?

☐ *Go!* — How does our Catholic faith make an observable difference in our marriage?

Date 161

☐ *Ready* — What did you like best and least about school?

☐ *Set* — Do the people you surround yourself with currently bring you happiness?

☐ *Go!* — Are you unable to relax because of an overwhelming internal sense of needing to be productive?

Date 162

☐ *Ready* — Which museum, city or historical landmark would you enjoy being a tour guide for the day?

☐ *Set* — What is the best and worst New Year's Eve you have experienced?

☐ *Go!* — When do you experience unexpected feelings of anger?

Date 163

☐ *Ready* — Do you have an ancestor you really admire?

☐ *Set* — Which of your birthdays has been the most special to you?

☐ *Go!* — Is jealousy hurting our marriage?

Date 164

☐ *Ready* — Do you like your given name?

☐ *Set* — What would you change about your work history?

☐ *Go!* — Which character traits did you inherit from your mother and father?

Date 165

☐ *Ready* As a child, did you have a cherished stuffed animal or lovey?

☐ *Set* Do you attract or repel drama?

☐ *Go!* Can you sometimes identify with the Apostle, Doubting Thomas?

Date 166

☐ **Ready** — What did you do with the money from the first paycheck you ever earned?

☐ **Set** — Is there something you did not notice at first about me but have grown to love?

☐ **Go!** — Have you overcome a fear?

Date 167

☐ *Ready* — How would you spend an extra $1,000 that could only be used on yourself?

☐ *Set* — What would have been your dream career?

☐ *Go!* — Is there something you are afraid to tell your parents?

Date 168

☐ *Ready* — What is the weirdest thing you researched online this week?

☐ *Set* — How is society promoting dysfunction?

☐ *Go!* — Do I tell you "I love you" enough?

Date 169

☐ *Ready* — What is the best and worst meal you have ever eaten?

☐ *Set* — About which things do you need to be more consistent?

☐ *Go!* — What is something you wish you could change about the life of your mother or father?

Date 170

☐ *Ready* — Would you be too embarrassed, as an adult, to chase down an ice cream truck?

☐ *Set* — How would you like to improve the company culture at your work?

☐ *Go!* — Do you believe God loves you just as you are?

Date 171

☐ *Ready* Do you have any eccentric relatives?

☐ *Set* What motivates you to succeed in your career?

☐ *Go!* With which family member do you desire to have a better relationship?

Date 172

☐ *Ready* — Did you ever skip a class in school?

☐ *Set* — When was the happiest I have ever made you?

☐ *Go!* — What is a treasured memory of your parents?

Date 173

☐ *Ready* — Did you have a favorite and least favorite board game, as a child?

☐ *Set* — What soothes you the most at the end of a tough day?

☐ *Go!* — How would the world be different if you had never been born?

Date 174

☐ **Ready** — What was on your mind when we had our first kiss?

☐ **Set** — During your childhood, were you praised more for your efforts or natural talents?

☐ **Go!** — Which friends have been with you through good and bad times?

Date 175

☐ *Ready* — On a scale from 1-10, with 10 being high, what is the highest level of physical pain you have ever experienced?

☐ *Set* — Is there any type of work you would like to do after you retire?

☐ *Go!* — Have you identified your root sin as being pride, vanity or sensuality?

Date 176

☐ *Ready* — How long is too long to wait for a table at a restaurant?

☐ *Set* — What bad habits have you overcome?

☐ *Go!* — Who taught you about the 'birds and the bees'?

Date 177

☐ *Ready* — Is there a rule you think needs to be broken?

☐ *Set* — Was there a year in your life that was your favorite?

☐ *Go!* — What was the worst phase of your life?

Date 178

☐ *Ready* — Did you pass your driver's test on your first try?

☐ *Set* — What is the best relationship advice you have ever received?

☐ *Go!* — Is there a physical action or gesture you find romantic?

Date 179

☐ *Ready* — What foods would you pack for the ideal picnic basket?

☐ *Set* — Is there something that never ends well?

☐ *Go!* — Do you have any concerns about our current financial situation?

Date 180

☐ *Ready* — Did you have any collections during your childhood?

☐ *Set* — Have you ever received an award?

☐ *Go!* — Are we doing anything that is keeping us from receiving grace from God?

Date 181

☐ *Ready*   Were you a teacher's pet?

☐ *Set*   What is the strangest experience of your life?

☐ *Go!*   Is there anyone you are struggling to forgive?

Date 182

☐ *Ready* — What symbol would describe you if you were a country?

☐ *Set* — Do you hunger for more excitement in life?

☐ *Go!* — Is it easy or difficult for you to admit when you are wrong?

Date 183

☐ *Ready*   What items have you lost on your past trips?

☐ *Set*   How traditionally 'normal' was your family?

☐ *Go!*   Have you ever benefited from constructive criticism?

Date 184

☐ *Ready* — Who taught you how to ride a bike?

☐ *Set* — Were you ever grounded as a teenager?

☐ *Go!* — What are 3 reasons someone should be friends with you?

Date 185

☐ *Ready* — When you were a child, did you ever build a fort?

☐ *Set* — Who is the most courageous person you know?

☐ *Go!* — What work do you think God is currently doing in our marriage?

Date 186

☐ *Ready* — Was there someone who had a crush on you that was unrequited?

☐ *Set* — Are you looking forward to any upcoming events or milestones?

☐ *Go!* — What was a defining moment in your life?

Date 187

☐ *Ready* — Did you ever have a lemonade stand to earn or raise money?

☐ *Set* — Would you rather be a student, employee or employer?

☐ *Go!* — What is something your parents taught you that you really appreciate now?

Date 188

☐ *Ready* — How do you respond in situations when someone tells an inappropriate story or joke?

☐ *Set* — Are you a pessimist, optimist or realist?

☐ *Go!* — What would you like us to do that we have never done?

Date 189

☐ *Ready* — Did you ever toilet paper a house as a prank?

☐ *Set* — As a couple, are we involved too little or too much at our church?

☐ *Go!* — Are you more afraid of failure or success?

Date 190

☐ **Ready** — How important is God in your daily life?

☐ **Set** — When did you learn the truth about Santa Claus, the Easter Bunny, and the Tooth Fairy?

☐ **Go!** — Are you ever too hard on me?

Date 191

☐ *Ready* — What embarrassing skill do you have?

☐ *Set* — Is there anything you know to be true today that you did not know last year?

☐ *Go!* — Have you ever felt rejected by me?

Date 192

☐ **Ready** — Which one of us is the pickier eater?

☐ **Set** — What is the most important rule or expectation in our home?

☐ **Go!** — Would you want me to remarry if you die first?

Date 193

☐ **Ready** — What statue would you create if you were a sculptor?

☐ **Set** — Would you be open to a job that paid less, but you were happier?

☐ **Go!** — What do I mean to you?

Date 194

☐ *Ready* — Did you enjoy climbing trees as a child?

☐ *Set* — What is the biggest leap of faith you have taken?

☐ *Go!* — Are you worried that our busy schedules have caused us to drift apart?

Date 195

☐ *Ready*   What is the oddest reaction you have received when wearing ashes on Ash Wednesday?

☐ *Set*   Is there a seemingly insignificant thing you heard as a child that has stayed with you?

☐ *Go!*   Which 3 items would you save if our home were on fire?

Date 196

☐ *Ready* — What one food item would be hard to live without?

☐ *Set* — Does change excite or scare you?

☐ *Go!* — What would you do if you were given 6 months to live?

Date 197

☐ *Ready* — What causes you to procrastinate?

☐ *Set* — Does our life need a pause or rewind button?

☐ *Go!* — What is a life-changing event you have experienced?

Date 198

☐ *Ready* — What 3 things would be hard to live without?

☐ *Set* — When was the last time you did something for the first time?

☐ *Go!* — Can you remember a time you cried happy tears?

Date 199

☐ *Ready* — What is the most unusual or funny thing that has happened to you on a trip?

☐ *Set* — Who can always count on your support?

☐ *Go!* — What is something you want to achieve before you die?

Date 200

☐ *Ready* — Would you make a good food critic?

☐ *Set* — What embarrasses you easily?

☐ *Go!* — How has God revealed Himself to you personally?

Date 201

☐ *Ready* — Who was your favorite childhood babysitter?

☐ *Set* — Did you ever run away from home?

☐ *Go!* — Do I need to seek your forgiveness for anything?

Date 202

☐ **Ready** — If money were no object, how would you design our dream house?

☐ **Set** — What is the best surprise you have ever received?

☐ **Go!** — Are our different views on money hurting our relationship?

Date 203

☐ *Ready* — Do you have a favorite and least favorite retail store?

☐ *Set* — Are there any social situations that make you nervous?

☐ *Go!* — Which year of your life would you like to do over again?

Date 204

☐ *Ready* — Is there something that you refuse to share, even with me?

☐ *Set* — What life experiences did you miss out on that you regret?

☐ *Go!* — As a teen, did you receive any parental advice that you wish you had not ignored?

Date 205

☐ *Ready* — What is your favorite thing to do on one of our dates?

☐ *Set* — Were you encouraged to be close to your extended family?

☐ *Go!* — Which of our shared religious activities are having a positive impact on the quality of our marriage?

Date 206

☐ *Ready* — Are there any predictable things about me that you really like?

☐ *Set* — Which person, living or deceased, do you think would give good marriage advice?

☐ *Go!* — Do you forgive and forget or forgive and remember?

Date 207

☐ *Ready* — What holiday would you like to create?

☐ *Set* — Is there a quality you always look for in others?

☐ *Go!* — Do you consider yourself to be more passionate or reasonable?

Date 208

☐ *Ready* — What is your favorite zoo animal to visit?

☐ *Set* — Who do you consider to be a real-life hero?

☐ *Go!* — What impact have our parents had on our marriage?

Date 209

☐ *Ready* — Who taught you how to drive?

☐ *Set* — What is the best compliment you could give a person?

☐ *Go!* — Is there anyone who frightens you?

Date 210

☐ *Ready* — Is there a movie that seriously scarred you?

☐ *Set* — What are the best and worst aspects about this time in history?

☐ *Go!* — In making decisions, what role does God's Word play?

Date 211

☐ *Ready* In what ways do you feel rich?

☐ *Set* When are you at your most productive?

☐ *Go!* Who influences you the most, me or your family of origin?

Date 212

☐ *Ready* — What would you name a new restaurant you opened?

☐ *Set* — Which board game reminds you of our marriage?

☐ *Go!* — During your childhood, were you overprotected or neglected?

Date 213

☐ *Ready* — How would you like to celebrate your 100th birthday?

☐ *Set* — What is overrated?

☐ *Go!* — Do you think it is too late to do certain things in your life?

Date 214

☐ *Ready* — What are your memories of your childhood neighborhood?

☐ *Set* — When was the last time you were out of your comfort zone?

☐ *Go!* — Are you living inside or outside your definition of integrity?

Date 215

☐ *Ready* — Do you have a favorite item in our home?

☐ *Set* — What has been impressing you most about me lately?

☐ *Go!* — Are we contributing an appropriate amount of money to the Church?

Date 216

☐ *Ready* — What is the best music concert you have ever attended?

☐ *Set* — How would you complete this sentence, "I used to think ___ but now I think ___"?

☐ *Go!* — What do you know about the lives of your grandparents?

Date 217

☐ *Ready* — Would you rather go parasailing, bungee jumping or hang gliding?

☐ *Set* — What makes you nervous?

☐ *Go!* — Do we have a loving ritual of connection as we begin and end each day?

Date 218

☐ *Ready* — What pep talk do you give yourself each morning?

☐ *Set* — Is there anyone you wish would write you a letter?

☐ *Go!* — What was the most challenging setback you have ever endured?

Date 219

☐ *Ready*   What is your least favorite word?

☐ *Set*   Are there times when it can be difficult to interact with you?

☐ *Go!*   What makes you angry at yourself?

Date 220

☐ *Ready* — Would you rather attend a Broadway play, the ballet or the symphony?

☐ *Set* — What is the biggest 'what if' on your mind?

☐ *Go!* — How do you like to spend time with God?

Date 221

☐ *Ready*   Do we share any common personality traits?

☐ *Set*   As an adult, do you ever give into peer pressure?

☐ *Go!*   What world events were significant to you, during your childhood?

Date 222

☐ *Ready* — What one adjective best describes me?

☐ *Set* — Are you a dreamer or a go-getter?

☐ *Go!* — Is there anything I have done recently that may have unknowingly hurt you?

Date 223

☐ *Ready*   Which singer reminds you of your childhood?

☐ *Set*   Are your opinions stronger than most people?

☐ *Go!*   What has been the biggest disappointment of your life?

Date 224

☐ *Ready*   What is the best and worst piece of travel advice you have ever received?

☐ *Set*   In what situations do you need to be more fearless?

☐ *Go!*   What makes you cry?

Date 225

☐ *Ready*   What how-to book could you write?

☐ *Set*   For what reason would you ever leave your current job?

☐ *Go!*   How has prayer impacted your life?

Date 226

☐ **Ready** — What bores you to tears?

☐ **Set** — Is there a big-ticket item that you purchased and regretted later?

☐ **Go!** — What are 3 of your strengths?

Date 227

☐ *Ready* — Where would you like to live for 6 months to learn a new language?

☐ *Set* — Who mentored you during your childhood?

☐ *Go!* — Have any of your dreams been dashed?

Date 228

☐ *Ready*   Would you like to ride a tandem bike with me?

☐ *Set*   Where do you see us in 20 years?

☐ *Go!*   What is something you are glad you will never have to do again?

Date 229

☐ *Ready* — What is the weirdest item you have ever purchased?

☐ *Set* — How do you best remember your grandparents?

☐ *Go!* — Did your parents tell you, "I love you" when you were young?

Date 230

☐ *Ready* — What extracurricular activities were you involved in as a young person?

☐ *Set* — Have you learned more from your failures or successes?

☐ *Go!* — How do you apply the Church's teaching on 'redemptive suffering' to your own suffering?

Date 231

☐ *Ready* — Who in your life do you wish you had met sooner?

☐ *Set* — Would you be willing to die for a belief or cause?

☐ *Go!* — Do I make enough effort with the people who are most important to you?

Date 232

☐ *Ready* — What are you better skilled at than most people realize?

☐ *Set* — Is there a memory that never fails to make you laugh?

☐ *Go!* — Have you ever experienced a betrayal?

Date 233

☐ *Ready* — Was there a high school class you thought was a total waste of time?

☐ *Set* — What was the best day of your life?

☐ *Go!* — Did you experience freedom to explore your interests during your childhood?

Date 234

☐ *Ready* — What scents or smells do others like but you dislike?

☐ *Set* — Where is your favorite place to spend time with me?

☐ *Go!* — Do you think we exacerbate each other's bad habits?

Date 235

☐ *Ready*   As a teen what fads did you embrace?

☐ *Set*   What is underrated?

☐ *Go!*   Would Jesus smile upon your efforts at evangelizing our Catholic faith?

Date 236

☐ **Ready** — What should the minimum age limit be to get married?

☐ **Set** — Did you party or study more as a teenager?

☐ **Go!** — What is the most important lesson you have learned thanks to our relationship?

Date 237

☐ *Ready*   What childhood T.V. programs did you enjoy the most and least?

☐ *Set*   When you talk about me to others, what do you say?

☐ *Go!*   Is there anyone in your life who tries to manipulate you?

Date 238

☐ *Ready* — Which holiday do you look forward to the most every year?

☐ *Set* — What criteria do you use to determine if you should trust someone?

☐ *Go!* — Do your parents tell any stories about you that you find upsetting?

Date 239

☐ *Ready* — What type of crowd did you hang out with in high school?

☐ *Set* — Is there a fundamental truth that you know with an absolute certainty?

☐ *Go!* — What one home remodeling project would you like to work on next?

Date 240

☐ *Ready* — What unsolved historical event would you be most interested in unraveling?

☐ *Set* — Is there something you have seen lately that made you think of me?

☐ *Go!* — How have you experienced the Holy Spirit moving in your life?

Date 241

☐ *Ready* — Is there a favorite holiday decoration you loved from childhood?

☐ *Set* — What do you remember most about our first road trip?

☐ *Go!* — When do you feel loneliness in our marriage?

Date 242

☐ *Ready*   How could you become more organized?

☐ *Set*   What are the three best decisions you have ever made?

☐ *Go!*   If we wrote a marriage book, what would be the title?

Date 243

☐ *Ready* — What do you like about where we live?

☐ *Set* — Is there a time of day you prefer for us to have serious conversations?

☐ *Go!* — When do you feel self-centeredness takes precedence in your life?

Date 244

☐ *Ready* Do you have a 'must have' travel item?

☐ *Set* Is there an achievement of mine that brings you joy?

☐ *Go!* How do we work well together as a team?

Date 245

☐ *Ready*   What is the shortest amount of time you have held a job?

☐ *Set*   Is there anything we can do as a couple to better the world?

☐ *Go!*   During difficult times, do you feel closer or further from God?

Date 246

☐ *Ready* — Are you happy with the amount of alone time we spend together as a couple?

☐ *Set* — What do you remember about your first significant injury?

☐ *Go!* — Is there anything we have not talked about but need to discuss?

Date 247

☐ *Ready* — What tasks would you assign to a personal assistant?

☐ *Set* — How was our first kiss memorable?

☐ *Go!* — Were you encouraged by your parents to talk about your positive and negative emotions?

Date 248

☐ *Ready* — What is the worst weather storm you have ever experienced?

☐ *Set* — Are there times you take me for granted?

☐ *Go!* — What are our strengths as a couple?

Date 249

☐ *Ready*   What is the hardest class you have ever taken?

☐ *Set*   How do you feel when I smile at you?

☐ *Go!*   Has anyone ever lost your trust?

Date 250

☐ *Ready* — How has your childhood hometown changed over the years?

☐ *Set* — Which 5 canonized saints would you like to greet you at the gates of Heaven?

☐ *Go!* — Do you believe I sometimes overshare about our marriage with others?

Date 251

☐ *Ready* — What is most satisfying about your job?

☐ *Set* — How would our neighbors describe our marriage?

☐ *Go!* — What was your first impression of my family of origin?

Date 252

☐ *Ready* — What is the best and worst customer service you have ever experienced?

☐ *Set* — How have you sacrificed for me and our marriage?

☐ *Go!* — Has anything surprised you about our relationship?

Date 253

☐ *Ready* — What is something that should be taught, but is not?

☐ *Set* — Do we have enough fun together?

☐ *Go!* — What do you think unforgiveness does to a person?

Date 254

☐ *Ready* — When it comes to clothing what is more important, style or comfort?

☐ *Set* — What has taken up too much of your life?

☐ *Go!* — Is there anything I could do to improve my relationship with your extended family?

Date 255

☐ *Ready* — What item would you be willing to stand in line for hours to purchase?

☐ *Set* — Who in the Bible, besides Jesus, do you try to emulate?

☐ *Go!* — Do you think you have enough healthy independence in our marriage?

Date 256

☐ *Ready* — What is the best and worst party you have ever attended?

☐ *Set* — Would you rather visit my parents, your parents or skip the visit all together?

☐ *Go!* — What area of our relationship do we need to work on most?

Date 257

☐ *Ready* — When was the last time you were pushed to your physical limit?

☐ *Set* — While spending time with others, do I still make you feel like a priority?

☐ *Go!* — What promises have you kept and broken in your life?

Date 258

- [ ] *Ready* — What was your favorite childhood toy?

- [ ] *Set* — With our marriage in mind, what advice would you give newlyweds?

- [ ] *Go!* — Who is hiding behind the mask you present to the world?

Date 259

☐ *Ready* What is the craziest thing you did when you were young?

☐ *Set* Have I helped to create a loving and warm home for us?

☐ *Go!* Are you consistently faithful in fulfilling your commitments?

Date 260

☐ *Ready* — What story or joke do you tell the most often?

☐ *Set* — How would you describe your own personal Heaven on earth?

☐ *Go!* — Does your life have a recurring theme?

Date 261

☐ *Ready* — Who is clumsier, you or me?

☐ *Set* — How rich would you be if you converted my love for you into money?

☐ *Go!* — What is your greatest fear?

Date 262

☐ *Ready* — Who is your favorite president?

☐ *Set* — What is the hardest paycheck you have ever earned?

☐ *Go!* — How can we strengthen our marriage?

Date 263

☐ *Ready* When do you feel most patriotic?

☐ *Set* What do you love most about your parents?

☐ *Go!* Are you satisfied with how we share household responsibilities?

Date 264

☐ *Ready* — Have you ever accepted a dare?

☐ *Set* — Do you owe an apology to anyone?

☐ *Go!* — What can lead you to feel sad?

Date 265

☐ *Ready* — What do you think your life would be like if you ended up with the career you wanted as a child?

☐ *Set* — When was the last time you felt really challenged?

☐ *Go!* — Have you ever experienced discrimination because of your Catholic faith?

Date 266

☐ *Ready* — How would you design a postage stamp?

☐ *Set* — If you could be anywhere in the world, where would you be and what would you be doing?

☐ *Go!* — What is the greatest accomplishment of your life so far?

Date 267

☐ *Ready* — What is something you are glad you did once, but likely will never do again?

☐ *Set* — Are you satisfied with who you have invited into your life?

☐ *Go!* — What is a treasured memory from the past year?

Date 268

☐ *Ready* — Is there an animal that overwhelms you with fear?

☐ *Set* — What would you consider to be a wasted life?

☐ *Go!* — Have you ever been given a prophetic word or image that resonated and then came true?

Date 269

☐ *Ready*   Is there a smell you would like to bottle?

☐ *Set*   What behavior do you refuse to tolerate from others?

☐ *Go!*   Have I recently done anything to make you feel disrespected in public?

Date 270

☐ *Ready* — Which room in our home do you enjoy the most?

☐ *Set* — When is the last time you felt genuinely proud of yourself?

☐ *Go!* — What important decisions have you based upon spiritual discernment?

Date 271

☐ *Ready*   What is the worst haircut or hairstyle you have ever had?

☐ *Set*   Do you prefer a male or female boss, or does it really matter?

☐ *Go!*   Would your younger self be proud of who you are today?

Date 272

☐ *Ready* Which shoe do you put on first when getting dressed, the right or the left?

☐ *Set* What are 3 things we have in common?

☐ *Go!* Are there any situations where you believe 'the end justifies the means'?

Date 273

☐ *Ready* — Would you rather be early or late to a gathering?

☐ *Set* — Is there something you always wanted to do as a child but never experienced?

☐ *Go!* — What is amazing about your life story?

Date 274

☐ *Ready* — What is the most expensive non-essential thing you have ever purchased?

☐ *Set* — How did we make each other smile this week?

☐ *Go!* — Have any of your lifelong dreams come true?

Date 275

☐ *Ready* Is there something other people do that you find amusing?

☐ *Set* What is the first thing you notice about a person?

☐ *Go!* How like Christ do you want to grow in your faith?

Date 276

☐ *Ready* — What was the first meal you ever prepared?

☐ *Set* — How does a person act that makes you instantly dislike them?

☐ *Go!* — Which moment from your past would you happily relive again?

Date 277

☐ *Ready* — Would you rather have more time or money?

☐ *Set* — What are the positive aspects of our marriage?

☐ *Go!* — Is there a goal I can help you to accomplish this year?

Date 278

☐ *Ready* — Would you rather have a personal chef, housekeeper or massage therapist on staff?

☐ *Set* — What are some of the little things I do that drive you a little crazy but that you secretly like about me?

☐ *Go!* — Do we spend enough time sharing our faith walk with one another?

Date 279

☐ *Ready*   Do you consider yourself to be a creative person?

☐ *Set*   Is there anything you would like to do more of together?

☐ *Go!*   What are you willing to struggle for in life?

Date 280

☐ *Ready* — Who do you wish lived closer to us?

☐ *Set* — What is the best and most difficult aspect of Lent for you?

☐ *Go!* — Was there anything your parents did not allow, but should have during your childhood?

Date 281

☐ *Ready* — Would you rather watch a sunrise or sunset?

☐ *Set* — What couple do you admire the most?

☐ *Go!* — How have we progressed in the goals we set for our marriage?

Date 282

☐ *Ready* — Have you ever been stuck in an elevator?

☐ *Set* — What skills do you envy in other people?

☐ *Go!* — Are there distractions that hinder your personal or professional productivity?

Date 283

☐ *Ready* — Is there anything you have been doing for years only to discover you have been doing it incorrectly?

☐ *Set* — When do you prefer to receive advice vs. just have a listening ear?

☐ *Go!* — What do you consider to be the worst crime against humanity?

Date 284

☐ *Ready* — Have you ever gotten in trouble for playing a prank on someone?

☐ *Set* — Who or what has made you the angriest?

☐ *Go!* — What is the best investment you have made in your life?

Date 285

☐ *Ready* — What is the first movie you remember seeing as a child?

☐ *Set* — Do you have a favorite outfit that I wear?

☐ *Go!* — How do you perceive Heaven?

Date 286

☐ *Ready* — What article of clothing have you owned the longest?

☐ *Set* — How is our life most exciting right now?

☐ *Go!* — Do your morals differ from your parents?

Date 287

☐ *Ready* — What would 10-year-old you think about your current self?

☐ *Set* — Who or what demotivates you?

☐ *Go!* — How have you changed since our wedding?

Date 288

☐ **Ready** — What natural phenomenon would you want to experience if safety was not a concern?

☐ **Set** — When do you feel emotionally connected to me?

☐ **Go!** — Are you obsessive in any areas of your life?

Date 289

☐ *Ready* — Are you self-taught in any subjects or skills?

☐ *Set* — How do I make you proud?

☐ *Go!* — What makes a person unforgettable?

Date 290

☐ *Ready* — What era would you choose to experience for one year?

☐ *Set* — How can I help you face your fears?

☐ *Go!* — What brings you the peace of Christ?

Date 291

☐ *Ready* — What do you consider to be the ultimate comfort food?

☐ *Set* — Are your priorities in order?

☐ *Go!* — What is the most memorable advice you have ever been given about life?

Date 292

☐ *Ready* — Have you ever overcome a phobia?

☐ *Set* — What is the best gift you have ever received?

☐ *Go!* — Is there anything I can take off your plate to lighten your load?

Date 293

☐ *Ready*   What is your dream car?

☐ *Set*   Are you able to confront someone who is mistreating a person?

☐ *Go!*   If you had 24 hours alone without interruptions, what would you do with the time?

Date 294

☐ **Ready** — In school, did you prefer to sit in the front or back of the class?

☐ **Set** — When you were growing up, were your parents affectionate with each other?

☐ **Go!** — How do you interact with someone who seriously disagrees with you?

Date 295

☐ *Ready* — What is one thing you never did in high school that you wish you had?

☐ *Set* — Were you a rebellious child or teen?

☐ *Go!* — How do you think you would react if you got to meet Jesus in Heaven?

Date 296

☐ **Ready** — Which T.V. program, past or present, would you like to be a guest star?

☐ **Set** — How can I be more present in our marriage?

☐ **Go!** — Are you able to set healthy boundaries with everyone in your life?

Date 297

☐ *Ready* Which phrase do I say most frequently?

☐ *Set* Is there something you wish I would ask you more often?

☐ *Go!* What keeps you awake at night?

Date 298

☐ *Ready* — How would you complete the following sentence, "What if there was a ___, that could ___?"

☐ *Set* — Is there a way you behave to be accepted by others?

☐ *Go!* — How do you determine what is moral or immoral?

Date 299

☐ *Ready* — What is your favorite and least favorite month of the year?

☐ *Set* — When do you know you can count on me?

☐ *Go!* — What gives you hope?

Date 300

☐ *Ready* — When you first wake up, how would you describe your mood?

☐ *Set* — Who is your favorite Catholic media personality?

☐ *Go!* — What were the major turning points in your life?

Date 301

☐ *Ready* — Which disease would you like to cure?

☐ *Set* — Do you still have a cherished object from your childhood?

☐ *Go!* — Would others describe your work ethic as laid back or untiring?

Date 302

☐ *Ready* — Is there a hobby you would like to try but have not had the opportunity?

☐ *Set* — What kinds of situations cause you frustration?

☐ *Go!* — Are your expectations for yourself and others too high or too low?

Date 303

☐ *Ready* — Who is more organized, you or me?

☐ *Set* — How often do your biggest worries and fears come true?

☐ *Go!* — What line should someone never cross with you?

Date 304

☐ *Ready* — What one word described you as a teen?

☐ *Set* — How would you spend a week in solitary confinement?

☐ *Go!* — If you had a friend who spoke to you the same way you speak to yourself, would you consider them to be a good friend?

Date 305

☐ *Ready* — Where would you bury a treasure chest?

☐ *Set* — Would any of your schoolteachers be surprised at your station in life?

☐ *Go!* — Are we faithful all week or just 'Sunday Catholics'?

Date 306

☐ *Ready* — Have you ever participated in a research study?

☐ *Set* — Is there a part of your life that you feel is on hold?

☐ *Go!* — What do you want your final words to be on earth?

Date 307

☐ *Ready* How does your ideal morning routine compare to your current morning routine?

☐ *Set* Where were the most popular hangouts when you were a teen?

☐ *Go!* Is there a person you wish you had not trusted?

Date 308

☐ *Ready* — What activity would you be willing to practice one hour a day to become exceptionally skilled?

☐ *Set* — How good are you at reading people?

☐ *Go!* — What would be the best version of your life?

Date 309

☐ *Ready* — Who is more forgetful, you or me?

☐ *Set* — If you had the nerve, what is something you wish you could say to people?

☐ *Go!* — What brings meaning to your life?

Date 310

☐ **Ready** — What sound annoys you the most?

☐ **Set** — Are we playful enough with each other?

☐ **Go!** — In our home, are we living out the scripture, "But as for me and my house, we will serve the Lord"? (Joshua 24:15)

Date 311

☐ *Ready*   What is the most exhilarating experience of your life?

☐ *Set*   Is there anything you are dreading?

☐ *Go!*   What childhood nightmare do you still remember?

Date 312

☐ *Ready* — What ability or skill would you like to wake up with tomorrow?

☐ *Set* — Is there something you find more difficult than it sounds?

☐ *Go!* — What is the most disheartening realization you have come to in life?

Date 313

☐ *Ready*   Is there a book that should be required reading for an engaged couple?

☐ *Set*   What was your role within your family of origin?

☐ *Go!*   In what area of your life do you need to exert more self-control?

Date 314

☐ **Ready** — What is the most impulsive thing you have ever done?

☐ **Set** — Are we investing our time appropriately in growing our marriage?

☐ **Go!** — Is there something you want or need more of in your life?

Date 315

☐ *Ready* — What is your favorite number?

☐ *Set* — Do you think you have any biases?

☐ *Go!* — Who is the most faith-filled Catholic you have ever known?

Date 316

☐ *Ready* — What makes you blush?

☐ *Set* — Who is the fictional character who closely resembles you in terms of attitude?

☐ *Go!* — What do you take for granted?

Date 317

☐ *Ready* — How was your birthday celebrated when you were a child?

☐ *Set* — Is there an important lesson you learned from a relative?

☐ *Go!* — What if anything would you want to change about our marital intimacy?

Date 318

☐ *Ready* What song makes you want to cringe?

☐ *Set* Is there an unsettling aspect of your life?

☐ *Go!* What are you most ashamed of from your past?

Date 319

☐ *Ready* — Which insect do you wish would go extinct?

☐ *Set* — What is your funniest high school memory?

☐ *Go!* — Did you have a sense of belonging in your family of origin?

Date 320

☐ *Ready* — Is there something that should never be joked about because of its serious nature?

☐ *Set* — What are your spiritual strengths?

☐ *Go!* — Do you believe you are making a difference in your community by the way you live your life?

Date 321

☐ *Ready* — If you were limited to only one type of clothing for the rest of your life, what would you choose?

☐ *Set* — What is the most ambitious thing you have ever attempted?

☐ *Go!* — Is there something you would want included at your memorial service?

Date 322

☐ *Ready* — Are you good in emergencies?

☐ *Set* — How would you complete the following sentence, "I wish I had someone with whom I could share ___"?

☐ *Go!* — What would you want me to know if it were my last day on earth?

Date 323

☐ *Ready*   What can you never get enough of in life?

☐ *Set*   How do you define success?

☐ *Go!*   Are your parents good at apologizing when they are in the wrong?

Date 324

☐ *Ready* — Which candy best describes me?

☐ *Set* — What is the biggest opportunity you have been given?

☐ *Go!* — Do you consider anything in your life as a great failure?

Date 325

☐ *Ready* — What act would you have as a skilled circus performer?

☐ *Set* — Is there something we should enjoy now because it will not always be available?

☐ *Go!* — What type of ministry would you like to start?

Date 326

☐ *Ready* — Did you ever play games of pretend as a child?

☐ *Set* — What question do you wish more people would ask you?

☐ *Go!* — Is there a time in your life when you felt used by someone?

Date 327

☐ *Ready* — If it were safe what exotic animal would you like to have as a pet?

☐ *Set* — What is your personal motto?

☐ *Go!* — When are you most comfortable in your own skin?

Date 328

☐ *Ready* — What fascinates you?

☐ *Set* — Is there something that touches your heart and restores your faith in humanity?

☐ *Go!* — Were you ever given a much needed second chance?

Date 329

☐ *Ready* — When do you lose track of time?

☐ *Set* — What brings out your sentimentality?

☐ *Go!* — Is there a risk you took that did not pay off?

Date 330

☐ *Ready* — Which of your funny habits might other people consider weird?

☐ *Set* — Do you think more people look down or up to you?

☐ *Go!* — What about me indicates that I am striving to be a saint?

Date 331

☐ *Ready* — What should we name our very own planet?

☐ *Set* — Are you sensitive to the needs of others?

☐ *Go!* — Were you spanked as a child, and if so, how old were you when the spankings stopped?

Date 332

☐ *Ready* — If you hosted your own talk show, who would be your first guest?

☐ *Set* — What burning question do you want answered?

☐ *Go!* — How are you like your parents?

Date 333

☐ *Ready* — If you were in trouble, besides me, to whom would you seek advice?

☐ *Set* — How do you cope when things are not going your way?

☐ *Go!* — What do we need in our life to make it more fulfilling?

Date 334

☐ *Ready* — What prop would you pay money for, from a movie or television show?

☐ *Set* — Do you consider yourself a good judge of character?

☐ *Go!* — How do you define a 'life well-lived'?

Date 335

☐ *Ready* Have you ever been the benefactor or recipient of a random act of kindness?

☐ *Set* What are your thoughts about the Saint Padre Pio quote, "Pray, hope, and don't worry."?

☐ *Go!* How do we bring out the best in each other?

Date 336

☐ *Ready* What would a T-shirt you designed say?

☐ *Set* How do you respond to unsolicited advice?

☐ *Go!* Were you taught to view sex as holy or dirty?

Date 337

☐ *Ready*   What would your crime be if you were arrested?

☐ *Set*   Is there something unusual that stresses you out more than it should?

☐ *Go!*   When could I have taken initiative but did not?

Date 338

☐ *Ready* — Is there a friend you have lost contact with that you would like to reconnect with again?

☐ *Set* — What is the one rule you have for yourself that you will never break?

☐ *Go!* — At what point in your life was your self-esteem the lowest?

Date 339

☐ *Ready* — What will we be doing in our 80's?

☐ *Set* — How can anyone self-improve?

☐ *Go!* — Do you have a strong need for everyone to like you?

Date 340

☐ *Ready* — As a child, which Halloween candy did you dislike receiving when you were trick-or-treating?

☐ *Set* — What is a happy memory of our marriage?

☐ *Go!* — When is a time you have felt the strong presence of God?

Date 341

☐ *Ready* — Where could we go for a romantic weekend?

☐ *Set* — What have been the most and least productive times in your life?

☐ *Go!* — Are your life dreams on hold, moving forward or backward?

Date 342

☐ *Ready* — Which ice cream flavor best describes me?

☐ *Set* — What is the kindest thing you have done for someone?

☐ *Go!* — Is there a bad habit you struggle to overcome?

Date 343

☐ *Ready* — What 3 adjectives described me on our wedding day?

☐ *Set* — Do you focus more attention on the people or things in your life?

☐ *Go!* — What is your number one prayer?

Date 344

☐ **Ready** — If you were a weather person, how would you describe me?

☐ **Set** — What is the funniest story about yourself?

☐ **Go!** — When have you felt the most courageous?

Date 345

☐ **Ready** — What do you consider to be the best food item at the fair?

☐ **Set** — Is there something you feel God is inviting you to do right now?

☐ **Go!** — What is your biggest regret?

Date 346

☐ *Ready* — What is the most embarrassing thing you have ever worn?

☐ *Set* — Are you in denial about a person or situation in your life?

☐ *Go!* — Is there anything you have asked me to do that I have neglected?

Date 347

☐ **Ready** — What is the weirdest thing that your family of origin does together?

☐ **Set** — If you could relive one hour of our relationship, which hour would you choose?

☐ **Go!** — How can I help you complete a bucket list item this year?

Date 348

☐ *Ready* Do you have a 'must have' to start your day?

☐ *Set* Who in your family has the best relationship?

☐ *Go!* What is the most dangerous situation you have survived?

Date 349

☐ *Ready* — Did you have an embarrassing or hurtful nickname during your childhood?

☐ *Set* — Would you marry me again?

☐ *Go!* — Do we live our marriage with passion and purpose?

Date 350

☐ *Ready* — Did you ever get lost as a child?

☐ *Set* — If you had an entire day to spend with Jesus what would you do?

☐ *Go!* — What makes us different from other couples?

Date 351

☐ **Ready** — Where is the most unusual place you have ever fallen asleep?

☐ **Set** — When am I at my sexiest?

☐ **Go!** — What have you done for the people you love?

Date 352

☐ *Ready* — If you became famous, would you relish the limelight or miss your privacy?

☐ *Set* — Would you sacrifice your life for a stranger?

☐ *Go!* — Who do you miss the most?

Date 353

☐ *Ready* — If you had $300 to spend on something special for me, what would you buy?

☐ *Set* — What have been the most peaceful moments of your life?

☐ *Go!* — Do you have any wounds or traumas from your past that need healing?

Date 354

☐ *Ready* — Is there a book you would like to see made into a movie?

☐ *Set* — How can I love you better?

☐ *Go!* — What is something that no one else knows about you, besides me?

Date 355

☐ *Ready* — What is your favorite time of day?

☐ *Set* — If you had a billion dollars, how would you use the money to benefit those in need?

☐ *Go!* — How do the Beatitudes guide your faith?

Date 356

☐ *Ready* — Is there anything you consider to be an absolute waste of time?

☐ *Set* — What inspires you?

☐ *Go!* — Do you lay your problems at the foot of the cross only to take them back?

Date 357

☐ *Ready* — What is something you would never compromise on in life?

☐ *Set* — Do you have any fears about getting older?

☐ *Go!* — Are you suffering in any way spiritually?

Date 358

☐ **Ready** — What is the most peaceful and restful night of sleep you have ever experienced?

☐ **Set** — Do you have any ideas on how we can improve our date nights?

☐ **Go!** — How do you view your mistakes and failures in life?

Date 359

☐ *Ready* — Who was your best boss?

☐ *Set* — What would you regret not doing in life?

☐ *Go!* — Do you feel you are putting in maximum or minimum effort into our marriage?

Date 360

☐ *Ready* — How do you respond when someone mistakes your Ash Wednesday ashes for a smudge?

☐ *Set* — What negative life situation did you turn into a positive?

☐ *Go!* — Is there an area you want to conquer where I can be more supportive?

Date 361

☐ *Ready* — Do you thank God for me every day?

☐ *Set* — Is the way you spend your time reflective of your priorities and values?

☐ *Go!* — What are some of your relationship goals for us?

Date 362

☐ *Ready* — What invention has most benefited mankind?

☐ *Set* — Is there something about you that you wish others understood?

☐ *Go!* — What question do you not dare ask your mother or father?

Date 363

☐ *Ready* — Do you ever rehearse a phone call beforehand?

☐ *Set* — What are the characteristics of a healthy marriage and are we a good example?

☐ *Go!* — Has God made you aware of some aspect of our marriage that needs attention?

Date 364

☐ *Ready* — Have you ever stayed up all night to watch the sunrise?

☐ *Set* — What is the greatest blessing I offer you as your spouse?

☐ *Go!* — Have I fulfilled your positive expectations of marriage?

Date 365

☐ *Ready* — What are some things you really like about me?

☐ *Set* — Can you name 8 things about our marriage that make you smile?

☐ *Go!* — What are your most treasured memories of our 365 dates?

Faith, Hope & Clarity

DANA NYGAARD

DANA NYGAARD is an expert in encouraging others to heal wounds and traumas that often block the extraordinary plan God has for their lives. She combines a master's degree in counseling, bachelor's in secondary education, and more than thirty-one years of experience engaging and motivating audiences across the country. Dana captivates and inspires others with her warmth, infectious humor, and down-to-earth approach. She is a cradle Catholic with a heart for the New Evangelization with training in healing and deliverance ministry.

Dana is a sought out motivational speaker who brings expertise as a Licensed Professional Counselor specializing in Cognitive Behavioral Therapy. Her extensive experience in marriage counseling and trauma therapy brings hope and healing to those who encounter her dynamic approach.

As founders of Cana Marriage Retreats, Dana and her husband, David, travel nationally, delivering a unique blend of proven psychotherapy techniques with authentic Catholic spirituality providing audiences with practical solutions that have life-changing effects. The Nygaards are the parents of an adult son and reside in Plano, Texas where Dana has a thriving private practice as a Catholic Psychotherapist.

For more information about having Dana
speak at your event, please visit her website:

www.dananygaard.com
Email info@dananygaard.com

Made in the USA
Columbia, SC
22 March 2022